THE TIP SHOP

Also by James Brown

Go Round Power Please (1995)

Lemon (1999)

Favourite Monsters (2002)

The Year of the Bicycle (2006)

Warm Auditorium (2012)

Floods Another Chamber (2017)

Selected Poems (2020)

THE TIP SHOP

James Brown

TE HERENGA WAKA
UNIVERSITY PRESS

Te Herenga Waka University Press
Victoria University of Wellington
PO Box 600 Wellington
teherengawakapress.co.nz

A catalogue record is available at the National Library
of New Zealand.

ISBN 9781776920105

Printed by Blue Star, Wellington

Contents

3

1

A Calm Day with Undulations

The sea is the greatest plain on Earth, I think
as I surf my bike down the shingle beach
and pedal away from the land.

It's a calm day with undulations.
My tyres flow freely
across the naval surface.

Half a league from shore
and the swell deepens.
I roll up and down each frequency.

Without barriers, wind increases over the sea.
I stop to hunker in the trough of a wavelength
—a lull where rainwater might pool briefly

before soaking in—and peer deep into the galaxy
of the planet. Shadows glint beyond sunlight.
Turn back now, they groan.

Never listen to whales.
I know where I am
going with this.

I know where
I am going
with this.

I know
where
I am

going
with
this

.

Flensing

They announced it as a 'flensing of the old sort',
which gave me pause and caused me to take stock

of who I thought I was and what I thought I thought I thought:
my backgrounds, ethnicities, gender percentage; loyalties, beliefs,

preferences—all my ones and noughts—and my portfolio
of course—in what was I invested?—and what in god's hell

would be my username and what would it be doing with its
screens and files on the proposed seating plan

as the tumbrel rumbled up and down the hedge-fund rows
beneath the fat, low-hanging laws and crows on scarecrows?

Collecting

You pick one up at the Tip Shop:
oblivion's final sieve meets your lucky day.

You get one on Trade Me, the only bidder
to spot it in a 'box of bits'.

One you find in the gutter between
Hy-Grade Diary and Flygers Line.

So that's—let's see?—five.
You had two already, see.

You rummage one at a school fair, gliding
easily between the phone-faced parents.

The Sally Army shop in Eltham has two.
Over-priced but, hey, it's for a good cause.

A couple are really hard to find. By the time
you see one, you're after something else.

Mr Spencer

As kids, we were scared of the old man
over the fence. With his old face and clothes,
he would march up and down behind
a big green lawnmower, scowling.

His look convinced us he was a bad lot.
He also had too many sheds, so we snuck over one day
to investigate. Inside were at least three lawnmowers,
which we knew at once he was smuggling.

I'd begun playing soccer, as it was called then,
and would practise by running up and down our garden
passing the ball off the corrugated-iron fence—down
using my right foot, back up using my left.

My dad encouraged the use of both feet.
I eventually became similarly able with either,
though not at all able at football. So of course
the ball went over the fence.

Normally, I'd check to see if old Spencer was about
before going to retrieve it. But today
he picked it up and cheerfully threw it back.
'You trying to do a balloony?' he bellowed.

I didn't know what a balloony was, but if you ever
need a metaphor for something—anything—
there it is. Balloonies, I've come to discover, are hard
to get right. This one's coming along though.

Logic Explained

Our teacher asked for
a show of hands. When we got
out the bath, did we

dry our lower or
upper half first? The upper
half was logical

because drying your
lower half first meant your wet
upper half would drip

onto your lower.
I dried my upper half first.
I was logical.

Pure Human Endeavour

God prefers drawn-out sports, like golf or cricket.
His hand may be seen in an endless tennis match
—tie-break after tie-break—his face in dog trialling.

He loves the Tour de France—three weeks, rest days,
and the shadow performance, ably enhanced
by Lucifer, His safe sleight-of-hand.

Tournaments and leagues give shorter sports a chance
to experience divine intervention and wrath.
But at the end of days, someone wins, someone loses,

making test cricket the apex of His
divine wisdom. Five days and then a draw!
Wonderful! Benevolent! Vengeful!

Oh, the supplication of the forward defensive stroke.
T20 is just having a laugh. He doesn't even watch it,
making it, perversely, an example of

pure human endeavour, along with
cheese-rolling, Ultimate Ninja Warrior
and truck racing from Nevada.

Their Feelings

Their feelings are like a mosquito sliding
its proboscis into a freckle. Their feelings are like
light through blinds in an 80s music video.
Their feelings are like techno under aurora in Norway.
Their feelings are like swimming in sunlit sea and
seeing a shadow. Their feelings are like when they've
taken bath salts that turn out to be bath salts, and they
end up in A&E and their mothers have flown in from
Hamilton and are holding their hands and crying, but
all they can think about is how their lives have become a
TV hospital soap which they could have been written out of
or out of which they could have been written.
Their feelings are like a Mindful Self Compassion course
when someone asks where the hyphen goes in the title
and the convenor says 'Anywhere' and the person says
'I don't think this is what I am looking for.'

Schrödinger's Wife

Mary didn't walk with us Sundays. She ran.
With earbuds, she could keep reading. Her shop,
Schrödinger's Books, was a tough mistress.
'Are you working today?' we'd ask. 'Yes and no,'
she'd reply. She just needed to 'finish the books'.
Can the books ever be finished? They wink at us
as though there are uncertain things
they think we ought to know.

After Mrs Far died, Mr Far continued to run
Island Bay Stationers. He opened erratically.
Some days the lights were off, the door open
and he'd be out back, grumbling to her about
the Möbius double-sided tape dilemma or the
unilluminating home planetariums—*See Marvels
of the Galaxy in the Convenience of Your Own
Ceiling.* 'Who ordered *those*?' a voice echoes.

Schrödinger had a child with his mistress
and ultimately set up house with them
and his wife. He then fathered daughters
with two other women. Of his thought experiment,
he wrote: 'The entire system would express this
by having in it the living and dead cat
(pardon the expression) mixed
or smeared out in equal parts.'

The Waiting Room

I'd been invited to a party. The rooms were dark and crowded and loud. Conversations were people shouting. I squeezed past and, off the kitchen, found a small room with chairs and a sofa by a coffee table with magazines. It was deserted. I sat down and picked up a magazine. John, an actor, walked in. 'What are you doing?' he asked. 'Waiting,' I said. He sat down. Someone else came in and John introduced us. 'I'm John. This is James. We're just,' he made a rolling motion with his thumbs, 'waiting.' Others came and went. 'Can't be much longer—James has been here ages.' I nodded and made a what-can-you-do? face. The scene played out over and over, with variations, until John suddenly stood up. 'Well, that's me,' he said, as if he'd just been called, and shook my hand. 'Good luck with everything.' Thirty years later, I sometimes see him on television, where he usually plays middle-aged men who drink and smoke too much.

Football Again

The attraction of football, of all sport really, is simplicity. The goal is nearly always a goal. Yes, teams park the bus, but if they happen to score, their fans won't complain. Beyond scoring a goal, the next best thing is to create or prevent one. If you're not doing one of those three things, your contribution will go unnoticed, which is most of life and just about fine. When I was a kid, however, I wanted to be good at football. I practised, but mostly by myself, which meant I got okay at controlling and kicking a ball, but not at dribbling round people or tackling. In games, I ran into spaces where, if the person passing the ball had also been me, I would've been put through. But they weren't. Instead, they turned the other way, beat their marker, and scored.

I Must Not

I must not skateboard
in the facility.
I must not do fartleks
in the facility.
I must not take song lyrics
seriously.
I must not sleep
on my back
if I'm going to
snore like a whore.
I must not borrow
other people's things
without asking.
I must not take
everything people say
personally.
I must not push Martin
in the trough.
I must not abuse
the ag bike.
I must not abuse
my screen time.
I must not make shuriken
in MIG welding.
I must not contribute
to the discussion
without being asked.
I must not hide
from the people
trying to help.
I must not keep
running away.

I Must

I must be prepared
to make sacrifices.
I must remove my
earbuds in class.
I must pay attention
to the people talking
to the group.
I must put the biscuits
on a plate.
I must have shoes
that I can polish.
I must remember
to bring my manners.
I must treat the cat
with respect.
I must keep it real
on my resumé.
I must eat breakfast.
I must own my own
actions.
I must recognise the signs
and take myself out
of the situation.
I must use my own
toothbrush.
I must save for
the things I want.
I must learn to
forgive people.
I must learn to
eat vegetables.

Resilience on Checkout 7

I am young and a bit shy,
which I agree is a shame.
I don't actually mind
the sound of my voice, I just
don't like people looking—at me,
at my uniform, which I
never wear right.
'Don't smock me,' say the fillers.
This is their joke and
I've thought up another one
but haven't said it in case it
comes out dumb.
It's hard to know how to say a joke.
Your voice has to be right,
but you can't really think about it
when you're saying it
like you can't really think about
being on checkout when you're
on checkout. The boss tells us
that wages are the biggest impact
on his margins so we need to
smile more because we are
his loss leaders.
It's like Thursday night netball
when I throw a bad pass because
I was too slow or too quick and threw
to where I thought someone was or
was going to be, but they weren't,
and a groan goes up.
Like—I know. I get it.
It's a bad feeling,
but I take it on board
because it's good to realise
when you've made a mistake.
Everyone's a bit useless sometimes,
though some people don't seem to realise it

or they don't let it bother them if they do.
They just carry on. I would like to know
how to be more like them.
You can always do things better because
there are always better ways
to do things.

Water Features

He'd lied to me so often, I no longer believed myself.
Did I really enjoy a late-night bath with candles?
Isn't that a lot of trouble to go to by yourself?

Listen to your body, people say.
My body seemed to be saying, 'Okay. Sure.
I can go with candles.'

Listening shows you more than looking.
Sometimes darkness is essential as oil—if you buy into
essential oils, which aren't, but isn't all life just marketing?

If you can't sell yourself to yourself, how can you . . . etc . . .
which sounds like desk-top calendar advice written by someone
who's maybe dabbled with candles and a water feature

but who's never been near going under,
who doesn't realise that baths are actually small boats
taking on water.

Lesson

When was the last time you
washed a green apple—peeling
off the irksome sticker—and
quartered it on a chopping board?

Then sliced the quartered cores out
with two fine v-cuts
and threw them onto the lawn
for the birds? Then cut each quarter

in half and passed the eighths
around, eating two yourself
—the sharp fresh taste sweeter
than you'd expected?

Post-colonial Studies

We admired a row of
renovated colonial houses.
'You know who lives in them?'
said my friend. 'Policy analysts.'

Insulation

My barber says that people no longer
being able to afford houses
is a no-brainer opportunity.
He turns on the shop's TV.
Cue the leafy suburbs. Cue the dawn chorus.
The tent of realty is specially crafted
to respond to inequity. Its breathable fabric
repels applicants arriving by bus
while allowing bond plus four weeks' rent
to flow out unchallenged.
I could go on about this, but I don't want to
ruffle feathers, so I just mumble how
buying a second house and renting it out
is a bit like dismantling a tree twig by twig
to build yourself a giant nest.
What's going to happen to all the baby birds,
especially our natives?
I don't know if I say this or think it
in the voice of someone from Forest & Bird
or whether my barber says it facetiously.
The voices in my head get muddled
with the voices in the world. Someone waiting says
Dawn Chorus and the Leafy Suburbs
is a drag act. Someone else waiting says
you know what's beneath those
Supremes' dance moves and spangly dresses?
The usual suspects. Wink wink. Someone waiting says
you know what'd solve the housing crisis?
Triangle rooms. My barber says
to stop the whining
put bananas in the diff.
No charge for the advice.
It's about Kiwis helping Kiwis.
He preens grey nodding heads
and sweeps up their locks
for the birds. That's a dead end,
if ever I heard one.

Cruelty to Animals

We got you so the children
could learn about looking after
something more vulnerable than themselves
—aged 4 and 6 as they were—
learn how to feed you and keep your
water topped up, and to let you
in and out when you wanted to go
in and out, which is frequently,
and to protect you and provide you
with affection. Which they did,
though I am sure there were times
when you, also, felt they didn't
quite get it right, particular
as you are. But now, like their
mother, queen of the dramatic
exit, they've left for bright new futures,
and yet here you still recline
—single, spayed, catered for—
your comfortable life stretching
beyond its natural expectancy.
Believe me, I understand about
coming to the end of usefulness,
the difficulty of continuing to make
a contribution, of not wanting to become
a burden. The days go on and on.
Soon it'll be Easter—a time when
sacrifices have always been made—and, sadly,
neither child will be home this year
to bestow the kind of unconditional love
you helped foster, which is going to be
absolutely devastating
for us both.

Trust Your Consideration

This is the place
where I have come to lose
a year of distress and sadness.
The spot where
part of my soul has been led
and has wept
in what has become
my back to the world's
toll, feeling
the rain and the sun
lost and lost.

Physicality reflects
expression.
Eyes close in anguish
or calm.
Control leans precariously.
Capture that
before letting go.

The edge offers surrender
to the elements, place
and clarity. The world
is open. Each of us
seem limitless. The tilt
of the open palm.

Arched listening.
Grace, the shape of a sail.
Text and skin and industrial nature.
Steel, concrete, wood, iron.
Emerging life on the surface
as if creating its own art.
A history of scars,
over which we have no control,
sways mercy over our lives.

Space and Time

The trees groan
and claw the weatherboards
as if to come inside.
Please . . . just one night of respite.

Room, table, window, chair . . .
The neighbour's dog barking
at nothing to speak of,
except perhaps suburbia . . .

tonight glazed by a supermoon,
its heavenly body fan dancing
between clouds, which wrap around like
backgrounds in the Hanna-Barbera cartoons

you used to watch, adrift between the soaps
mid-afternoon . . .
You try not to look too hard
at what changes and what

keeps going past . . . 'like sands
through the hourglass' . . . 'three or four hills
and a cloud' . . . Wile E. Coyote noticing
he's stepped onto nothing . . .

Top stories tonight:
A just-launched Mars probe
is experiencing colder
than expected temperatures.

You thought space always close
to absolute zero, but of course
Sun proximity must count, like
the sunny rooms in your flat that

cost more, which is why you're
up against a hill staring into
Antarctica—shingle, ice blink, swell—
a place that trains astronauts for

a possible mission to Mars
because it provides ICE
(Isolation and Confinement
in an Extreme Environment).

Perhaps you could apply?
June, July, August . . . the sun
barely visiting. You transform yourself
via CV. In Case of Emergency

use Image Correction and
Enhancement. A BA means
you can walk on water, on air.
On nothing.

The Crystal Halo

I take a late-night walk by the sea, the suburb drawn
in on itself, the roads at long last long
stretches of empty space like
dreams you can't remember.
The Milky Way glows with phosphorescence.
What is this, some kind of poem?
I'm the sort of person who can spot but not pronounce
the Magellanic Clouds. Well, most of the world
is unsayable, I tell myself for the umpteenth time
in my tongue-tied, misaligned life.
I locate the Southern Cross
and work out south—for all the good it does me,
as if I'll ever navigate by starlight—
and hope for shooting stars and satellites.
The flat sea barely brushes the shore, a faint
smell of woodsmoke settling upon it.
Then I see her, ankle deep.
She's wearing a black dress . . . or
could it be some sort of swimwear?
Is this a midnight dare? No one else is there.
No towel. No bundle.
It's winter. I'm some way off.
She stands, facing into the darkness.
I think in circles, symptoms.
I'm there for her. I'm here for you.
We're at the end of the Earth.
None of us knows what to do.
Eventually (probably about
five minutes), a line of drizzle
floats through
and I turn for home,
the last streetlight forming
a crystal halo.
Yes, easier to end a poem.

2

The Great Employee

I got a job as a night-filler at a local supermarket.
      We'd arrive as it closed at 5:30 each evening
and clock in. I loved the way the machine punched
      the time onto the cardboard slip with my name on it.
My area was the deli, which was slightly complex
      because the products had to be rotated
so the freshest yoghurts and cheeses were at the back.
      The deli was a chilled room, which customers
had to enter and exit. I wore my jersey and fingerless wool gloves,
      but still needed to step out to warm up.
The supermarket was in an old warehouse with the stock
      stacked high above the aisles, and which we
accessed by scaling industrial stepladders.
      Health and Safety was a green first-aid cabinet.
Stock had toppled, but I don't think a customer had ever
      actually been struck. At least not directly.
The day-staff comforted them and some sort of discount
      would be offered. The supermarket was
independent and cheap, and had done well, so well that
      we soon moved to new, purpose-built
premises. I was amazed—it looked like a real supermarket.
      The deli items were now on refrigerated shelves
and all the stock was stored safely out back.
      But we still clocked in and out.
I was given a new role. I had to start half an hour
      before the others, assess each aisle
for what was required, then go out back, fill the pallets,
      and wheel them into place before
the others arrived. They were mostly overseas students,
      studying business. Bhagat was the senior guy.
At first I thought I'd got the new role on merit—my
      meticulous rotation of best-before dates
not going unnoticed—but in fact the others had lectures
      and simply couldn't arrive before six.
I was wondering about going to uni, and so paid close
      attention to them. The only guy

not doing business had one side of his head shaved
      and impressed me by juggling
three big-sized cans of baked beans. He was in
      his final year of some ology I'd
barely heard of. 'What are you going to do?' I asked,
      looking for answers. Beneath our hands
Cameo Crèmes were outselling Melting Moments.
      'Get a job,' he said.
The night boss was Mr Quinn, a grizzled Aussie
      who sometimes had his young son in tow.
They would prowl around, trying to catch us eating
      whatever had 'accidentally' burst open.
We worked the aisles in pairs. My preferred partner
      was a skinny guy about my age.
Non-work-related talk was growled at, so we'd
      developed a system of mimes and grins.
One night Quinn and son rounded a corner just as we'd
      stuffed our mouths with Tangy Fruits.
We froze, cheeks ablaze. I thought we were
      set to be sacked, but Quinn just
bawled us out, while his tubby kid gawped
      like a guilty guppy. Another time
I yanked the pallet jack too sharply
      and three boxes of glass-bottled vinegar
peeled off. The stain spread across the
      smooth, pristine lino, oozing beneath
each aisle, so that even in my horror and
      self-pity I thought, I wonder what this
looks like from above? and recalled
      a morning milk round with my friend
Stephen Foley when he decided to show me
      how to do a 'slide'.
He pushed our trolley at full speed towards
      a patch of loose gravel, then turned
sharply. I can still see the tyres grip
      and try to make the turn,
the flipped trolley frozen briefly in mid-air,
      its 100 one-pint bottles gently exiting

the doomed craft to begin their various trajectories
        toward the false suburban footpath,
whose loose stones, which would've made it
        awkward to skateboard on,
had nonetheless proved insufficiently slippery
        for the slide I never got to see.
Spilt milk aside, surprisingly few bottles broke.
        It was the same in the supermarket, except
the smell of vinegar rose like sulphur. Some day-staff
        leapt into action with a massive
vacuum cleaner thing that sucked up everything, including glass,
        while I mopped the floor in shame.
But my co-workers were gentle. They understood breakage,
        leakage, the fine margins of error.
I saw camaraderie and wanted to belong somewhere,
        so for some weeks I kept asking the big boss
for a fulltime job. Then suddenly I landed one
        in a miserable shop just around the corner.
It closed at 5:30, then we had to cash up, so I'd
        scream over on my bike, clock in 15 minutes late,
and rush to fill the pallets. Sometimes the night crew were
        already waiting as I wheeled the last ones out.
Sometimes they came out back to help. It was no big deal.
        The shelves got filled. I didn't understand the world
beyond my world. My clocked-in lateness had come
        to the pay people's attention because
my first half hour was officially at normal rate,
        but the rest was at time and a half.
'I want a word with you,' the boss said one day,
        as I rushed in. 'If I've time,' I called,
running to my locker. I had pallets to fill.
        I flew back, buttoning my smock.
The boss stood in the centre of the loading bay.
        The departing day-staff hung back.
Bobo, my day-equivalent, didn't swap smiles.
        'You're late,' the boss said.
I explained about my other job and cashing up,
        that I always got here as fast as I could

and stayed to work my three hours. 'I pay you
          to work from 5:30 to 8:30,' the boss said.
'I work extra at time and a half,' I pointed out, 'but I
          don't mind it being paid at normal rate.'
No, that didn't bother me. I was a great employee.
          'Give me your smock,' the boss said.
I still didn't get it. 'But what about the pallets?'
          Bhagat was already doing them.
'Not your problem. Get your stuff and go.'
          I walked back to my locker. I gathered
the clothes from my miserable new job.
          I walked back across the loading bay.
I walked out the big roller door and unlocked
          my bike from a downpipe.
I pedalled away. Sodium light spilled
          like milk from the loading bay.
Soon Quinny would lower the door
          for security.

Oral History

Mid 1980s—synth pop, new wave,
      Flying Nun—and
I was hitching back to Palmerston
      from Auckland
with Robert. I suspect I'd been
      hanging out with
Izzy, a woman I didn't quite
      fancy enough.
Something about her laugh.
      She said her sister
—a surf lifesaver at Muriwai—
      got the looks,
which was, unfortunately, true.
      There's no denying
beauty. But, let's keep being honest,
      beautiful people
are usually completely horrible,
      though that
doesn't make the rest of us
      particularly nice.
Ugly Izzy was fun
      to go to gigs with
and, this visit, we even did a
      rubbish radio show
together on bFM. It was never
      going to go anywhere.
I saw her a few years later in DIC
      (a Palmy department store),
and she, quite rightly, ignored me.
      But back to the story.
Someone, possibly Izzy, dropped
      Robert and me
at the end of the motorway
      and we adjusted ourselves
on the littered verge, stuck out
      our thumbs and

faced the music. We stood
          a few hundred metres
apart (because people aren't likely
          to pick up two males),
with Robert first (because he wore
          glasses and a shirt).
The plan was that if he got a ride,
          he'd ask if the driver
would also take me. If or when
          we became separated,
we'd race. This scheme got us to
          Hamilton, then
Tokoroa. But, unlike the
          Palmy–Wellington hitch,
it was slow going and I knew,
          standing on the
long drag out of Tokoroa in the
          tilting afternoon sun,
that it would take a miracle ride
          to make Palmy
before nightfall. Another hour,
          and a car stopped
for Robert—its window framing
          his shrug as he
sped by. The cars whanged me
          into understanding
that no one had actually
          picked me up
that day—my rides were all
          courtesy of Robert.
Seed pods popped in the heat.
          I thought of bodies
in the scrub—how every other
          murderer was
a scrub-cutter from Tokoroa.
          You think that's
unfair? Go stand out there.
          Plan B: I retreated to

the Newmans stop and got a bus
          back to Hamilton
in time to catch the overnight
          train. Genius.
The carriage was almost empty.
          A backpacker opposite me
smiled and came over.
          She was Canadian,
just arrived, and on her way to
          friends in Wellington.
She asked how old I was. I bumped
          myself up to 22,
guessing, correctly, that I needed
          maturity. We drank
wine from plastic cups in the
          dining car, talked
about ourselves and assessed
          our reflections.
In the night carriage, she did
          what she could
under our blankets, top undone,
          rubbing against
my knee. 'The most exciting thing
          is not-doing-it'
Andy Warhol once wrote.
          The toilet was
discussed, but neither of us was
          up for it there.
We pawed each other through
          the Raurimu Spiral
and desolate level crossings in
          the heartland's
darkness until Palmy dawned
          in the window.
Parting was a hurried exchange
          of addresses and a
kiss like a quick-licked stamp
          for a letter

neither of us would ever write.
           I can't remember
her name. More importantly,
           I can't remember
whether I walked or taxied
           back to the flat.
Probably walked, after all Robert
           couldn't have made it
back yet. Surely. But there he was,
           sleeping peacefully.
He'd got his final ride on the
           glowing forecourt
of a Tūrangi service station
           just before it flipped
Sorry We're Closed to the night,
           thanks to two nuns
(and a pack mule, I wanted to add)
           who'd dropped him
right at our door. I related my
           experience with the
horny Canadian, but it seemed
           already unreal,
even to me, like a failed letter to
           Penthouse Forum
with insufficient multiple orgasms
           and one too many
'Honestly, this actually
           happened.'

Trigger Warning

Frances phoned from
    the far side of the museum:
'James, can you please
    come quickly, Frith's
not very well.' Panic rose
    and fell me back 25 years
walking to town through a
    grass-meets-gravel suburb
where a boy ran over the camber,
    his voice speaking up to me:
'Can you please come and help,
    my mother's not very well.'
I followed him across
    the quiet road to a
small wooden garage
    closed onto the street.
He showed me in the side door.
    His mother sat slumped
in the driver's seat. I turned
    the engine off and lugged her
outside, telling the boy
    'Phone for an ambulance—111.
Tell them where to come.'
    Her mouth was clamped shut.
I breathed in, sealed
    my lips around her nose
and exhaled. Her chest rose
    and fell. I began swimming, turning
my head for air, blowing hard into
    deep water. The surface came
and went, came and went.
    Her chest rose and fell, rose
and fell. The boy returned
    and asked if she was going to be
all right. I kept swimming.

The boy returned and asked
how she was. 'Not good,' I said,
	stopping to thump her chest
like Hawkeye on M*A*S*H.
	I may have said 'Come on.'
Her mouth was shut clamped.
	I sealed her nose with
my mouth and breathed out.
	The boy returned and said
something about something.
	Her chest rose and fell, rose
and fell. That was good. Air
	was going in. She was inflating
and deflating. Soon she would
	start. The grass turned
purple. At some point, a tall man.
	She would start soon.
Her chest rose and fell, rose
	and fell. Was that good?
The nose valve covered.
	The grass thin purple.
Soon, a tall man, the dad,
	appeared and said
something terrible like
		'Oh no.'
The boy arrived. He may have
	said 'Come on.'
And then the ambulance.
	Good. She would soon
start. The grass was purple
	and horrible. Soon.
The paramedics tried
	to prise her mouth
with a metal spatula.
	Her clamp was mouthed
shut. They connected a
	heartbeat monitor.

The grass green line was thin.
    They cut open her top,
held gelled paddles
    to her chest. Come on.
'Clear,' said one. The other
    raised his hands and
sat back on his knees.
    Her body flinched.
The thin green line was straight.
    They upped the voltage.
            'Clear.'
The straight green line was grass.
    They both sat back, slack.
Her shut was clamp mouthed.
    The boy and dad stood off.
Neighbours stood off.
    I said how her chest rose
and fell, rose and fell, so
    they gave me another go.
I placed my lips around her nose
    and poured myself in.
The air is going into her
    stomach, they told me.
I had to give a police statement.
    No, I hadn't noticed the
plastic tubing the policeman
    laid out across the table.
I was driven to a grand house
    to give a statement to
a coroner, who thanked me
    and returned to his dinner.
Then I was free to continue
    my trip into town, to a pub,
to pick up references from
    workmates, before catching
the overnight train to Auckland
    and a plane to England

for my big OE, giving me
plenty of time to stare
out the window at hydraulic
systems' manifestations,
cloud islands, and an all night
red light on the end of
a wing.

3

Water Cooler Bubbles

The dominant come in long lines
over the horizon

humming their horrible tunes
thumping their terrible tubs.

It was what it was
and it is what it is, et cetera.

You have to play the cards
that you are dealt, et cetera.

And you think I am referencing
large past injustices

but I am speaking about
a small thing

that happened at the water cooler
this morning.

The Breather

What's a breather again?
A useless guy. They just hang with the boys.
Do they go to uni?
Well, they enrol.
Can a girl be a breather?
I've literally told you this already.
I literally don't always get things first time.
You literally don't.
Is that a no?
Yes.

What's Your Name?

For my sister

—Pania.

—*OK Tanya.*

—No, Pania. With a P.

—*Pioneer?*

—Pania.

—*Pannier?*

—No. *Pa*nia, as in *pa*nini, but ending in A.

—*Paninia?*

—No. Like Narnia, but with a P.

—*Napier?*

—Um . . . it's famous in Napier. You know the Māori legend?

—*Nēpia? The All Black?*

—Let's go back to Tania. But with a P. At the front.

—*Ptanya. OK. What's your last name?*

—Brown, no E.

—*Brownoey. Got it.*

The Simple Hand

The simple hand occurred in a
club duplicate competition.
Everyone made 3NT; not one
defender made life harder for
the declarer . . .

Every West led Q♥. Declarer counted
three spades and two hearts.
If the diamonds did not produce
four tricks, South would try to score K♣.
Fortunately for the declarers, they all
made four diamond tricks easily.

Winning the lead in dummy, 2♦ was led and,
when East followed low, South played J♦
and this held the trick. Declarer cashed K♦,
on which West played 6♦ and East 10♦.
Then, 7♦ was led, West played 8♦ and
dummy rose with A♦, crashing East's Q♦.
Dummy's 9♦ was now good and secured
the contract.

What did the defence do wrong?
Good players will know immediately;
those less experienced may be perplexed
—but East told the declarer how to play
the suit. Let's replay the diamonds.

2♦ from dummy with J♦ in hand. With
the finesse succeeding, South knows East
holds Q♦—and East knows South knows.
When K♦ is cashed, instead of playing 10♦
—a card which no one knew East held—
East must drop Q♦. With J♦ gone, Q♦ and
10♦ are the same value, but dropping Q♦
now looks as if this is East's last diamond.

Declarer should now play 7♦ and, when
West follows low, insert 9♦ from dummy.
This loses to East, who tries not to smirk.

Play the card you are known to hold,
not one that should remain a secret.

Liking Similes

Here, the cicadas sing like Christian women's choirs
in a disused cotton mill.
　　　from 'Letter from the Estuary' by Erik Kennedy

When I hear cicadas, their singing always reminds me of
Christian women's choirs in a disused cotton mill.
I picture the conductor's arms bent in supplication
as she tries to draw forth the correct cicadian rhythm
from the collective rasp of Christian women.
Now her arms fall to her sides like the wings of a
cheap clockwork cicada made by Team Happy children
on a tymbal treadmill in China.

'The acoustics are wrong,' she says. *'Perhaps*
we need to try this someplace else. Yo,
what about that cotton mill down the road?'
So down the road the Christian women troop,
like a group of aspiring DJ cicadas in the flightless,
nymph stage of their life cycle, eager to graduate and
test their turntymbalist skills and scratching mettle
on some Technics SL1200 wheels of steel.

'Yes, we should have thought of this. Thanks.'
The cotton mill's machinery hums and clanks
like a shift of red-eye cicadas banging their tymbals
against the thickness of two short planks.
The Christian women file out
across the thread-stretched floor and
over the road to a conveniently
disused cotton mill next door.

'Hang on a minute. Just one
Christian women's choir may be insufficiently strong.
These are cicadas we long to imitate. Let's invite
some Baptist, Lutheran and, maybe, Presbyterian
women to unite with us in song.'

And so it comes to pass that the massed tymbals of several
Christian women's choirs fill the disused cotton mill
like a flock of rhetorical cicadas ascending Mt Improbable.

*'It's nearly there, but . . . I'm sensing there may be
some among us who are questioning their faith.'*
A small woman tymbals awkwardly, like a cicada nymph
trying to break out of its skin, and scuttles for freedom.
Then another woman stands and walks
calmly through the confused cotton mill
like a Tibetan Buddhist cicada
shamelessly swinging her tymbal.

*'Now I'm getting a low note, a tone beneath
the vocal range of the common Christian woman
and, it goes without saying, the common chorus cicada.'*
I raise my tymbal in public confession and remove my wimple.
Only male cicadas produce the distinctive cicada sound,
and only for courtship purposes, but this is hardly
a defence, nor does it prevent Christian women's choirs
from uniting in innovative mimicry attempts.

So honesty and gender force me to
vacate this adventurous simile at the
crucial moment, unjust minutes before it
reaches its unique potential in a disused cotton mill,
where the Christian women's choirs finally syncopate
their trilling ululations and handmade tymbal shakers
into rhythmic tonal twerks sounding not unlike
cicadas.

War and Design

The 20th century was mostly about two things:
war and design—particularly the design of chairs.
A lot of sitting needed doing in the 20th century,
especially as people got better at war.
Take, for example, the curved, modernist chair
Christine Keeler posed on at the start of the Cold War
in a shoot intended to promote a film about
her scandalous affair with John Profumo,
the British Secretary of State for War.
Yes, it looks like the classic Danish Model 3107
designed by Arne Jacobsen in 1955, but is in fact
a cheap 60s knock-off that photographer Lewis Morley
had Keeler wrap herself around because
she was reluctant to pose naked.
The handle hole in the plywood back
(a ploy to avoid copyright infringement)
is the most obvious sign it's not a genuine 3107.

Conflict and design braided and upbraided Keeler's life
as she sold and resold her story, which begins in poverty.
At age nine, she is identified as suffering from
malnutrition and sent to a health camp.
She despises her stepfather, who tries to
kiss her, saying he loves her not her mother.
In 1962, an ex-boyfriend fires shots at a house
where she is seeking refuge. There are babies.
The first, when she is 17, lives just six days.
Two other children, from two short marriages,
are called James and Seymour, which I only mention
because those are also my names, which makes me feel
uncomfortable. When asked, in 1980, what she will bring
to her new job as personal advice columnist
for *Men Only* magazine, she seems at a loss.

There is so much to say, so much
people don't want said. Her protector and connector

Stephen Ward, dead by his own hand in '63
at the conclusion of his trial for immorality offences
involving her, is found guilty *in absentia*.
Lord Astor expires three years later, a broken mannerism.
Yevgeny Ivanov, her ex-lover and former Soviet attaché
and spy, is discovered dead in his Moscow flat in 1994.
But Mandy Rice-Davies' 'slow descent into respectability'
glides right through to 2014. Well, it would,
wouldn't it? That's an in-joke. Stay with me.
Because Profumo lives until 2006, and Keeler till 2017,
thus ushering our love affair with war and design
safely into the new century.

Margins

For Ewen Coker

Even Ewen wasn't quite sure it was the right place when we dropped him in the darkness. I remembered him from Massey doing some endless unfinished thesis on Sanskrit. Now he'd bought a small piece of land outside Blackball and lived alone in a tin shed with no power, subsisting off his veg garden. His eyes widened when he talked about being kept awake all night by rats and possums running over the roof. It was so cold in winter, he said, some weeks he never warmed up.

The only other Blackball resident I've met was on the ferry. He looked like a young Hagrid and was paying off a house while collecting the dole. He was travelling north with a toy he'd found at a tip to present to a new baby he was meeting. It was a small, plastic, ornamental turtle. Not quite a choking hazard.

Even Steven

My flatmate Roger Stevens took me boulder rolling. He was a Smooth Earther, one of a small group of civil engineers dedicated to levelling the Earth. We climbed a hill, kicking rocks and scree behind us. 'You're an Erosionist,' I said. 'Erosion is a natural process,' he replied, 'and, yes, we encourage it.' 'But doesn't the land end up in the sea?' 'We redistribute earth onto low-lying areas to raise them up. Equitable height benefits everyone.' 'Not goats. Goats like hills.' 'Goats like anywhere.' 'Are you for land reclamation?' 'Yes.' 'What about harbour loss?' 'There's still a lot of sea to sail your boat on.' 'So your ideal planet is a flat expanse?' He laughed. 'We're Smooth Earthers, not Flat Earthers.' 'A marble, then.' 'The sea can keep its depths. Usable land without steps, switchbacks, viaducts and tunnels—what's not to like?' 'No views.' 'Build a tower.' 'What about water? It needs to flow downhill.' 'Of course. Gently. Controlled. Evenly distributed. We're not anti-gravity.' 'What about the majesty of mountains?' 'What about the overcrowding and hunger beneath them? And beneath you, perhaps.' He was starting to make sense. Together we levered an enormous boulder into the valley below.

Extended Object Label

A former Te Papa chief executive used this damaged Parker Ingenuity pen while overseeing a period of change at New Zealand's national museum. After his abrupt departure, the pen was found in a hidden drawer, along with three Curiously Strong Mints and a severed finger (origin unknown).

The Ingenuity combines the classic look of a longboard with the precision and smudge-proof flow of a skateboard. Parker Pens claim it does not leak from pressure, impact or temperature. The tip adjusts to the user's individual riding style.

This label is pitched at a reading level called '14-year-old boy'. Te Papa wish to grow the youth audience without losing the life-long learner; to attract people who wouldn't normally go to a museum. Help me, I'm being held hostage.

James Brown Is LARGE

Poor James Brown. He is normally
such a *live wire*, but today
he has not got out of bed
on the good foot.
He wanders about looking for
his *groove*, but he cannot find it.
Perhaps he left it in his dressing room
after last night's *super-bad* gig.
Or in the late-night cab back
to the hotel. By now
some *young punk*
will have picked it up
and run off with it
all the way to the
top of the hit parade.

Poor James Brown is late to rehearsal,
and has to fine *himself.*

James Brown is approached to feature
on a song by the *hot new thing.*
It could be an opportunity to reach
a new young audience
who are too *stupid* to know
about MR DYNAMITE.
It could also be
humiliating. He listens to a
rough cut of the track.
It is truly *awful.*
I do *not* feel good
about this, he thinks.

No one understands his new
material. His manager says
the new groove sounds *generic*
as if it's *sampled.* Which it is.

'Say *WHAT*?' exclaims James,
slapping his bouffant.
'It's *MY* sample! I'm sampling
MYSELF.'
'Exactly,' says his manager.

In the end, he just has to record
one of his *trademark screams*
for the *hot new thing*.
The song is about her abusive
boyfriend. Her producer inserts
the *scream* where her boyfriend
starts knocking her around.
In the song. The song
'*featuring* James Brown'.

In tonight's encore of
'Please, Please, Please'
James Brown is overcome by exhaustion:
the endless *rehearsal* of exhaustion,
the endless *performance* of exhaustion,
the endless *literature* of exhaustion.
He falls to his knees and Bobby Byrd
drapes a towel over him
and helps him from the stage.
The band keep going, waiting
for him to reappear,
which he does, but only because
he is a *true professional*,
and because it is *in his contract*
that he will die years later of
'complications resulting from
pneumonia'.

Regrets. Why did he support
Richard Nixon? Why did he support
Ronald Reagan? Because he ain't nobody's

lapdog. James Brown is LARGE. He *contains multitudes.*

The song '*featuring* James Brown' enters the Hot R&B/Hip-Hip chart at NUMBER ONE.

Ancestors

Ancestors are deceased people who
bother you sometimes. Like
crazy Great Aunt Unice, who
didn't let being dead stop her
expressing an opinion. It's
freaky, but ancestors are not zombies or
ghosts. Well, they're sort of ghosts. They might
haunt you,
if you've done something bad,
just to teach you. But they
kind of care, too.
Like, they don't want you to
muck up. It's like
noogie, noogie, noogie—hug!
One day our
pet cockatoo
Queen E, whom no one
really listened to anymore,
started talking in
the voice of Great Aunt
Unice, saying 'Take me to the
vet, take me to the *vet*,' and
when we did, the vet's
X-ray showed Unice's long lost wedding ring!
Your ancestors know things. Queen E survived the
zircon extraction, but eventually fell to indigestion.

Focus Freya Focus

Angela asks about
Bella's black Burmese
cat. Creepy Curtis crude comments.
Dream-on, dropkick. Don't distract
everyone. Eyes
flicker. Friendly fire? Focus Freya focus.
Gotta get good grades. Get
happy—ha ha.
Inquiry—I'm into it. I imagine
joy's jewelled
karma keeping
life level, like literally
moving me, my mum
nearer. No negativity,
our options opening out.
Pipedreams? Prayers? Perhaps
quiet
ruminations r relevant . . .
small spells
to tend
unicorns, unleash ultra-
violets. Verily,
we witches will wither writing
exercises, exams, exasperating
Y-chromosomes—yellow, yeasty, yacht-rock
zucchinis.

Hovercraft

'A baby can't drive,
especially Frank's goddamn hovercraft,'
I jabbered.
'Kids love movement,
not orbiting parents' quibbles,'
retorted Sue. 'Terrific U-turn velocity!
Well executed young zygote!'

Zig-zagging yawing expletives, we veered
under the subtext's redacted qualms, punctuated
oddities, nefarious manipulations.
'Language's knitted jersey,' I hmphed,
going for everything
divided couples believe
afterwards.

'Airborne babies can't decelerate evenly,'
Frank gesticulated. 'Hovercrafts insulate juddering.
Keeping level matters.'
'No, ours perambulates quirkily,'
replied Sue.
'The usual variants won't extinguish
yonder zygote's

zaniness.' Your ex's words vex.
Unexamined, their sugary reasoning quietly persuades,
only nothing matches.
Lovelorn kids juggle intermittent
homes, gyrated families.
Embryonic divorces concoct
babbling abecedaria.

My Final Football Game Poem

My boots fell apart
halfway through. Nevertheless
I soldiered on like

a man of letters.
At fulltime I displayed my
broken boots to

teammates by way of
explanation. 'Bad workmen
have bad tools,' said Gordon.

Agatha Panther

The furball in her lap stood up.
Clean up her act . . . or just *clean up*?

The manager with bandy legs
hung her coat upon his peg.

The other girls sat whispering
as Agatha unloosed the string.

'Never work with animals
or children' is an old stage rule.

A close shave with fur (genuine)
had the punters leaning in.

French stiletto nails and claws
gave Health and Safety sudden pause.

The man who caught her feather boa
used it to shoulder floss in Goa.

Winston Peters

Winston Peters was all there,
his cufflinks waving in the air.

His double-breasted pinstripe suit
cut a swathe and cocked a snook.

He palmed a coin to get us in.
His smile never left his grin.

Winston Peters had the rub
of bowling green and Cossie Club.

He said that he had little choice
if snowflakes settled on his voice.

'They're taking everything you owned.'
The Rita Angus frowned and groaned.

'Only fools,' he would repeat,
'test the water with both feet.'

He made whoopee more than amends,
but Winston Peters was my friend.

Alleged Female Orgasm

This time Dr Alfred Kinsey postulates
the AFO as a mare ridden bareback
along a desolate shoreline.
He clings to her mane as she clip-clops
out of the controlled environment and
across a grassy area toward the event
horizon. Sea air 'perks' her to a canter
and Alfred's lab coat opens in the breeze.
Using the latest CGI developed by Weta Digital,
he deploys a stupendous simulation, manoeuvring it
to part the mare's waterfall tail. We record
her chestnut flanks straining like similes
as she surges into a gallop, each rolling motion
perhaps agitating the possible source of the AFO,
the existence of which so divides us;
we who follow in large SUVs, some on
the edge of their seats, some by
the seat of their pants. Horse and rider leave
the grassy area and fly onto the open beach
and along the spumy edge of the waves. Faster, faster
into the salt haze of measureless distances buffering
to sun-squint white. There is no definition
in either direction, only the endless waves
running up the smooth face of the beach chasing
the AFO's thunderous hooves and the wind's roaring
forties. Alfred tries to hold on, tries to hold on,
the AFO on the tip of his tongue, the edge of his vision,
until everything—sun, sound, scent, theory—blows
to white infinity. When we catch up, Alfred
is sprawled on the beach, the chestnut mare
grazing quietly in the distance.
The AFO has once again eluded us.
Does it even exist? Is it a rainbow we've imagined
in the palms of our hands? Alfred's next theory is
the AFO might be a butterfly circling weightlessly

the Sea of Tranquillity. We're going to need
a rocket. The team at Weta Workshop
are up for it.

Dog Owners

You've got a new friend. He's talking to you.
He's just saying hello. He wants to play.
He can smell food from miles away!
Isn't he bouncy? He's only a puppy.
He won't hurt you. You startled him.
That's just how dogs dry themselves.
He wants you to throw it. *Good boy.*
He loves new people. He's very licky.
He's a great guard dog. They were bred to fight.
He's not even fully grown. He wants to sit there too.
He's not doing any harm. He's just doing his business.
Don't touch him. He doesn't like being patted.
He's not good at letting go. Come here George.
Drop it George! Drop it! *George!*
No George! *No* George! *No!*
He's never done that before.

An Explosion of Tears and Snot

Don't talk to me about Caps Lock until you've
seen the group chat. Don't talk to me about
common sense until you've done jury duty.
Don't talk to me about the unaffordable living
wage until you've paid my rent. Don't talk
to me about hard work until you've been
unemployed. Don't talk to me about the RMA
until you've lived downstream. Don't talk to me
about red tape until you've peeled it from my
lawyer's mealy mouth and clicked send. Don't
talk to me about level playing fields until you've
walked the sectioned land. Don't talk to me
about immigrants until you know where I'm
coming from. Don't talk to me about cyclists.
Just don't. Don't talk to me about love and its
crazy *raisons d'être* because love is always, in
some baffling way, French. Don't talk to me
about pain until you've curled up on the clifftop.
Don't talk to me about privilege because there is
no silver spoon, I mean lining, I mean bullet.
Don't talk to me about gridlock because I saw the
sleek features of the status symbol I'm driving
swoop the ad's digitally enhanced emptiness and I
bought it. Don't talk to me about the shocking
things you've just read. Don't talk to me about
anything. Are you listening? Can you hear what
I am saying?

Self-reflection

Cloudy with a chance of rain: a good day
for a brood, so I went out into the world
to see if someone would be mean to me,
because there are a lot of mean people
in the world and I would inevitably encounter one,
and, sure enough, when I got on the bus
the driver wasn't happy that I didn't have
'anything smaller', and even though my hand and voice
held only one sad note, I could see his point;
it is 'nonconvenient' (a word I'd heard recently
and I try to keep up) for a bus driver to count
out change; though the last time I checked,
hard-copy cash was still an accepted metaphor for
predetermined values and exchangeable for goods
and services, including a bumpy grumpy bus ride.
(Intake of breath)
Happily for my brood, the moment 'triggered'
—and this is a word I have come to embrace—
a time when I was really hungry (and I mean really
diabetic hungry) and tried to buy ten donut holes,
only to discover I had forgotten my wallet (actually,
I hadn't forgotten my wallet, I'd forgotten my pocket;
that is to say, the pocket within which my wallet was
safely ensconced, but it amounts to the same thing)
so, at the front of the queue and within range of sugar,
I tried to exchange the first thing of value I saw I had,
which was my watch, for ten donut holes.
(Recollective pause)
It wasn't an expensive watch, but it was still a good watch,
a goodish wind-up old-school watch, and easily worth
ten donut holes, but the guy pointed to his wrist,
which was already heavily encumbered by his own flashy,
and I would say inferior, digital watch (probably waterproof to
300 metres—like, *useful*) and said he already had one—*Well,*
not exactly I wanted to point out, but I was
too busy going hungry and low in my blood sugar

and my life, so the ensuing episode at the front of the queue,
from which I was unceremoniously jostled
while still trying to compute what to exchange
for sugar, was distressing and confusing to me,
and later in the ambulance something started
beeping, and I thought it was my watch,
or the guy's watch, despite both options being
unavailable, and that maybe I was underwater
losing sight of the day's themes, which, it says here,
were vulnerability and resilience.

Waiheke

You yearn so much
you could be a yacht.
Your mind has already
set sail. It takes a few days
to arrive

at island pace,
but soon you are barefoot
on the sand,
the slim waves testing
your feet

like health professionals.
You toe shells, sea glass, and odd things
that have drifted for years
and finally
washed up here.

You drop your towel
and step out of
your togs, ungainly,
first
your right foot, then

the other
stepping down
the sand
to stand
in the water.

There is no discernible
difference
in temperature.
You breaststroke in
the lazy blue.

A guy passing in a rowboat
says, 'Beautiful, isn't it?'
And it is. Your body
afloat in salt
as if cured.

Notes

'Trust Your Consideration' is an erasure poem using text from 'Proposal for *Solace in the Wind*, a sculpture by Max Patté 2007'. I deleted words and, in some cases, individual letters and repunctuated. The poem was commissioned for the Sonicity Sculpture in Sound project (www.sonicity.nz). The recording uses fragments from this and another poem I wrote based on the sculpture, which is the bronze man leaning into the wind on the wharf by Te Papa.

'Space and Time' features the opening four words of 'Room Table Window Chair' by Jenny Bornholdt. '[L]ike sands through the hourglass' comes from the opening theme to the US soap opera *Days of Our Lives*. '[T]hree or four hills and a cloud' is from 'Of the Surface of Things' by Wallace Stevens.

'The Simple Hand' is a found poem using text from 'Bridge' by Paul Mendelson, *FT Weekend*, Saturday 26 March / Sunday 27 March 2022.

'Dog Owners' is essentially a found poem.

Acknowledgements

Particular thanks to Catherine, whose gracious support enabled me to write this book. Grateful appreciation to Anna (especially for the cover advice) and Tessa (especially for 'The Breather'). Gratitude to Alan Gregg for advice, the Winston Peters quote and 'The Simple Hand'. Thank you to my unique sister Pania, who has experienced much of 'What's Your Name?'. Thank you to Claire Orchard for the poetry conversations. Thank you to Andrew Clarke for the football wisdom in 'Football Again'. Thank you to Erik Kennedy for letting me unpack his simile in 'Liking Similes', and to Fiona Gibb for the second half of 'Margins'. Thank you to Ashleigh for astute editing, selection and sequencing advice. And thank you once again to Fergus for ongoing belief. Thank you to Bill Manhire. Thank you to Russell Kleyn for the wonderful photos. Thanks to all at Te Herenga Waka University Press for helping the book into the world. And thank you (*you*!) for reading.

Thanks to the editors of the following outlets where some of these poems, or versions of them, first appeared: *Best New Zealand Poems 2018, Glottis Zero, More than a Roof: Housing, in poems and prose, New Zealand School Journal, NZ Poetry Shelf, POETRY Magazine, Sonicity: Sculpture in Sound*, and the Friday Poem on *The Spinoff*.